MEMOIRS OF A THATCHING FAMILY

1860 - 1968

Memoirs of a

Thatching Family

1860-1968

by

B. S. Reeve

The Larks Press

Published by the Larks Press
Ordnance Farmhouse
Guist Bottom, Dereham, Norfolk NR20 5PF

Tel: 01328 829207

March 1995

Printed at the Iceni Press, Fakenham

Cover Photograph:
Left to Right: Tom Reeve, John Reeve, Les Reeve, Bert Reeve.
The photograph was taken by John Topham Ltd. of Sidcup,
Kent in 1952 whilst the Reeve family was working on
Frog's Bottom.
The publishers have tried without success to find the owner of
the copyright of this photograph and those on p.51.

British Library Cataloguing-in-Publication Data
A catalogue record for this book is available from the
British Library

ISBN 0 948400 26 9

Author's Preface

After leaving school at the age of 12, and 53 years of hard manual labour, I do not pretend to be a 'writer', but I have roughly put together old accounts, estimates, extracts from old books, and true happenings during over a hundred years of a thatching family, so that some of the craftsmanship etc. may not be forgotten.

B.S.Reeve

Editor's Note

I believe that Eric Fowler (Jonathan Mardle) was one of the first people outside the family to read these memoirs. He was much taken with them and persuaded Margaret Langley, then working with the Norfolk Rural Industries Committee to try to find a publisher. She gave Mr Reeve some help with collating his typescript, but at that stage she had no success in finding a publisher and for many years the memoirs remained in store. Last year, when Mr Reeve was 94, she approached the Larks Press who agreed to publish as soon as was possible, so it is largely due to her perseverance that this interesting record of a thatching dynasty has appeared in print. I am also most grateful to Mr Reeve's daughter, Mrs Joan Matthews, who has allowed me to make use of her father's papers and photographs.

Sadly Mr Reeve died in September, 1994. He knew that his memoirs would be published, but was not able to see his words in print. Because he has not been available to be consulted, it has seemed right to leave his text virtually unaltered with the exception of a few amendments to punctuation. The special Norfolk flavour of these memoirs remains and the personal voice of the man who wrote them.

Illustrations

1. Peter Reeve of Bridgham

These extracts from old thatching account books, diaries and estimates, begin with a copy of an account in 1860 when few work people could, or did, put their accounts in writing. Therefore there are very few references to Peter Reeve of Bridgham, my grandfather, who died in 1905.

Nov. 1860   Sir Thos. Sebright, Bart.   Bridgham

To Peter Reeve, Bridgham, Thatching Doe Cottage

36 square yards at 5d per yd	£0.	15.	0.
22 feet Roofen at 5d per foot	0.	9.	2.
Brotches	0.	8.	0.
Rope for binding	0.	1.	6.
Allowance Money	0.	2.	0.
	1.	15.	8

Settled 16 May 1861

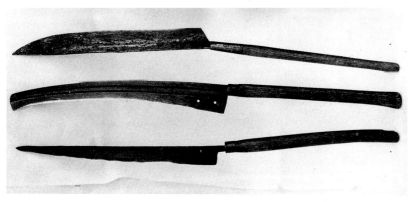

1. Thatchers' Knives
Top to Bottom: Ridge cutting knife, eave cutting knife for
straw thatching, flew or end cutting knife (1920)

April 1862   Geoffrey Humphrey   Bridgham

To Peter Reeve for thatching cottage   £   s.   d.

	£	s.	d.
Yards 74 at 4d per yard	1.	4.	8.
Roofen 16 feet at 4d per foot		5.	4.
Brotches 7 bunches		7.	0.
Binding hooks 3 doz		4.	6.
	2.	1.	6.

Settled May 3. 1862

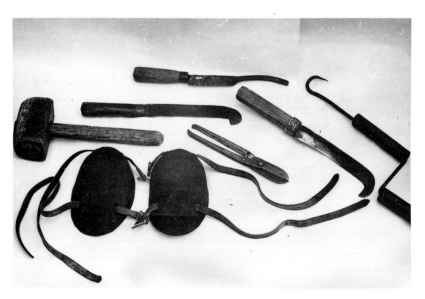

2.Thatcher's mallet, sharping hook, brotch riveing hook, sharping hook, bond twister or scud winder, pair of kneelers, wire cutters.

2

April 1886   Mr Ferguson, Farmer, Brettenham

To Peter Reeve, Bridgham

Riveing 41 bunches brotches	13.	8.
Getting brotchwood	1.	0.
Boy horse leading	1.	0.
Settled	15.	8.

[The boy was Tom Reeve, aged 10 and a half.]

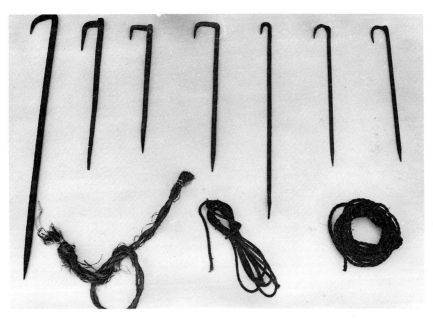

3. Thatcher's binding hooks of various lengths and ages.
Grass rope (18th century) , tarred rope of different ages.

Dec. 1886 Mr Ferguson, Brettenham, Norfolk
    Cottage thatching

High part one side,   9 yds 2 ft x 4 yds
Low part 2 sides   6 yds 2 ft x 4 yds
1 and a half days to mending & stripping

                                    Settled £3   5   3 $\frac{1}{2}$

*****

Feb. 13, 1866   Sir Robert Buxton

To Peter Reeve, Bridgham

For straw thatching Rushford Church.   Self and boy

	£	s	d
19 days work at 3/6 per day	3.	8.	3.
3 days riveing brotches		10.	6.
58ft Roofing at 6d per foot	1.	19.	0.
2 stone Rope for Binding at 7/- per stone		17.	6.
Allowance Money		10.	9.
2 Binding Hooks			6.
Settled	7.	6.	6.

Note the error in 'Roofing' price which apparently went through unnoticed. 'Roofing' (Roofen) is Ridging.

'Riveing Brotches' is splitting hazelwood into sizes for use.

'Allowance Money' is Beer Money.

Modern thatchers may question the use of only two hooks used during nineteen and a half days thatching on Rushford Church. This was because the thatch was bound on with tarred rope and the needle was 'threaded' from inside by a boy whose only access was through a hole in the roof. The two hooks were used when this was finally thatched over.

4

Beer allowance was a regular item in Peter Reeve's accounts, and some of the old stories we heard in later years seem to prove he used his 'allowances' and more at times.

When brother John and I went to thatch in villages in which Peter had worked, we were often asked, 'Do you stand on your "hid" (head) on top of the house like your grandfather did after he had been on the beer?'

He was thatching at Wretham when Mr Gayford, a farmer and landowner, came to see him at work. Mr Gayford perhaps doubted whether Peter was putting on the required thickness, or pulling enough of the old thatch off. Anyway he told Peter he wanted to come up the ladder. Peter promptly fastened his tools at the top, and without another word came down the ladder, and went off to the local pub - Wretham 'Stone Brigg' it was always called, but it was officially the 'Dog & Partridge'. Peter stayed for a while, and Mr Gayford wanted to know what was wrong. Peter replied 'Nothing, but there don't want two damn fules on the ladder at the same time.'

However, he was considered in the district to be a great craftsman and was usually preferred to some of the chaps who he described as 'straw throwers' who put the thatch on rough and thin.

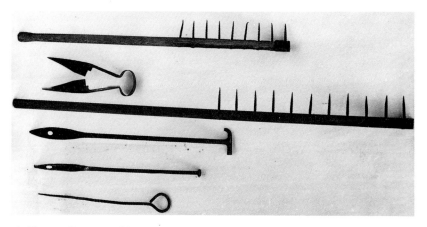

4. Top to Bottom: Short ridging rake, trimming shears, long rake for straw thatching, binding needle with hammer end, binding needle, plain needle.

5

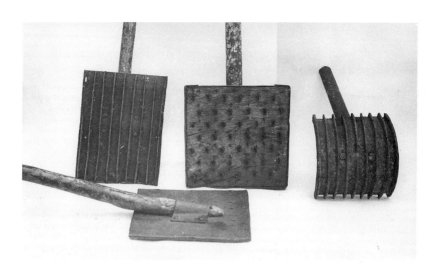

5a. Left to Right: Blacksmith-made iron leggett with bars, wooden leggett with flattened horse nails for roughage(1890), valley leggett, iron leggett showing back.

5b. Left to Right: Back of iron leggett, back of wood leggett, back of valley leggett, front of iron leggett with bars.

6

2. Thomas Reeve of Bridgham

My father Thomas Reeve was born at Bridgham and was naturally a thatcher from boyhood, as were his grandfather and other ancestors centuries back.

There were thatchers in nearly every village in those days, along with blacksmiths, wheelwrights and shoemakers. Competition was keen and the reward small, but there was always the feeling of a little independence by having a trade in reserve when other work was scarce. Father was born in 1875 and worked with Grandfather (Peter Reeve) whenever there was thatching available and on any other job that came along when thatching was slack. This usually happened during the worst weather of the winter, and Father sometimes joined a threshing gang, visiting various farms with the steam engine threshers, and during this time would be booking up orders and good thatching straw.

He had an advantage over many of the lads of his generation who left school at an early age. He took long courses of further education by post from an uncle in London and this was a great help to him in later life when he took part in public work, including Parish Council, Church Council, Founder Secretary of Bridgham Flower Show, Correspondent for Local Papers, Secretary-Treasurer of the Norfolk Reed Thatchers' Association, and committee member of the Norfolk Craftsmen's Guild.

Many of their thatching jobs were out of the village and they had long walks to work. There were no footpaths or short cuts that they did not know of in their walks to Croxton, Wretham, Hockham, Thetford, Attleborough and Rushford. The same routes were usually taken when they later had a pony and cart.

Father's first big job on his own account was in 1898 when he reed thatched Rushford Church, previously mentioned in Grandfather's account for 1866, and his work can be judged by the fact that it was 1951 before any major repairs were required.

*6. Rushford Church, straw thatched by Peter Reeve in 1866,
reed thatched by Tom Reeve (standing in foreground) in 1898,
repaired by Bert Reeve (left) and John Reeve (right) in 1951.*

Extracts from later accounts:-
June 1902   Hockham Estate
   Half Coating - Hanton's Cottage

To Thomas Reeve, Bridgham

	£	s.	d.
99 yds @ 5d	2.	5.	4
27 feet Roofing at 5d per ft		12.	4.
1 days work each, stripping etc.		7.	0.
Paid	3.	4.	9.

Half coating means the new thatch is laid about 6 inches thick
without stripping all the old off, instead of the usual 12 inch coat after
stripping off all the old.

Oct 9/1902   West Harling Estate

To Thomas Reeve, Bridgham   £   s.   d.
Half Coating Stable at Thorpe Farm

	£	s.	d.
163 yards at 5d per yard	3.	14.	8.
49 ft roofing at 5d per foot	1.	2.	5.
1 day stripping for 2		7.	0.
Paid	5.	3.	2.

* * * * *

Feb & March 1903   Mr J. Musker, Shadwell

Riveing 118 bunches brotches @ 4d   1.   19.   4.
                     Paid

9

March & April 1903   West Harling Estate
            Sir Edmund Nugent, Bart.   West Harling

To Thomas Reeve, Bridgham

     Riveing 118 bunches brotches @ 4d   1. 18. 8.
                     Paid

*****

April 1903   W. R-Rought, Brandon, Suffolk

Reed thatching Summer-house   £2. 15. 0
                           Pd

*****

May 1904   Thomas Reeve, Bridgham
         Shadwell Estate
Reed thatching Lych Gate at Rushford Church

33 fathoms Reed	£1.	15.	9
Carriage of same from Wroxham			
to Harling Rd Station	1.	0.	0
Straw for roof		9.	0.
Hooks for binding		11.	0
Brotches		5.	0.
7 days work @ 8/- for 2	2.	16.	0
	6.	16.	9

*****

1905
    West Harling Estate

Brotch riveing 11 days, self & boy
148 bunches @ 4d   £2.   9. 4
                 Pd

*****

Feb & March 1903   Mr J. Musker, Shadwell

Riveing 118 bunches brotches @ 4d   1. 19. 4.
           Paid

*****

Feb & March 1909   Sir E. Nugent, Bart., West Harling Hall

To Thomas Reeve, Bridgham

Riveing 174 bunches brotches @ 4d   2. 18. 0.
           Paid
[This was 21 days work. B.S.R.]

*****

Oct 19 and 20 1909   Miss Owles, Brandon, Suffolk
Thomas Reeve, Bridgham,
    To repairing summer House and
    fixing wire netting on top   9. 0.
    Brotches   10.
    Train fare and lodgings   5. 2.

              Pd.   15. 0.

Langmere Lodge on Shadwell Estate near Thetford, which Father thatched in 1907, took pride of place among his jobs and the photo of the finished roof was on his bill-heads and stationery for many years.

I include the following accounts because they are the only records of heather thatching in our books.

April 1912   T. B. Colman, The Manor, Bridgham

To Thatching Summer House with Heather	s.	d.
and cutting Heather	13.	4.
Cutting Reeds for lining	1.	8.
Boy	1.	0.
Paid	16.	0.

July 1912 To Thatching aviary & cutting Heather

Paid   7. 6.

7. Langmere Lodge on the Shadwell Estate, near Thetford, 1907.

Father employed other help before we were old enough to work. The first boy I remember was Walter Deacon, one of a large family. His father was a railway ganger and they lived at a Railway Gatehouse at Roudham on the A11. (The house and crossing have disappeared and been replaced by a bridge.) The Deacon family outgrew the house so much that sleeping quarters were rigged up in the garden with old pickled railway sleepers the main materials. On a hot night the smell of creosote was nearly stifling. Walter left thatching to work on the railways and lived at County School. He retired a ganger but he used his thatching experience to good effect, thatching corn stacks for the local farmers in his spare time.

Jack Ludkin from East Harling we remembered not so much for his work but for his skill with the mouth organ. He would often be heard playing on the way to work in the mornings. Nobody knows if he played on the way home after a hard day at straw-pulling. A visit from him at Xmas was a great treat for us kids.

Sid Bloomfield had the reputation of being late for work and an account kept by father in 1910 shows several short days. He suited us youngsters because he was always good for a 'lark about,' but he got severely wrong when he pushed two of us into a full water cart. He later moved to Yorkshire.

Henry Cutter left Bridgham school while I was a younger pupil, but I knew him well. He left thatching and went into private service and was a footman at West Harling Hall before being called up for the army 1914-18. When he retired he was a bank manager in South London.

Herbert Stammers was best remembered. He lived next door and was a small-holder and let out horses and traps, also a two-horse waggonette for various outings and Quoit Club away matches. He lost three fingers in a steam saw accident, which left him with only the forefinger and thumb on his right hand, which must have got awfully raw although he wore a thatcher's thimble on that finger at times. He died at Roydon near Southwold in May 1970 aged 91.

There was always plenty of thatching on the Shadwell Estate which stretched from Thetford Nunnery to Harling Road Station in length and from Illington to Barningham in width during the early 1900s. The owner the late Mr John Musker was known as 'The Squire' and it was most local labourers' ambition to work on his estate because of the privileges received if lucky enough to hold their jobs. The usual farmworkers' wages were 12/- per week, but at Shadwell they were paid 16/- with house rent-free, good cottage and free firewood. Mr Musker was also the first 'master' that I knew to pay family allowances, and supply bicycles to special workmen. Another generous gift came at Xmas when everyone working on the estate received a joint of beef. I think it was 4 lbs each for man and wife and one for each child. As Father worked there thatching at various times of the year he made certain he qualified for the beef at Xmas.

Yet for all these kindnesses 'The Squire' could be a tyrant. I have known him to tour the estate in a bad mood and sack twenty or thirty men for no apparent reason, in fact I was one of the victims, but it was possible to return there to work after a few months and many did so. Others spent a life-time on the estate.

My brother-in-law, Alf Meek (we married two sisters), was one of these, and in 1968 he received the super premier award for long service, 60 years, at the Royal Norfolk Show. Yet he only just escaped the 'sack' in his younger days. He was supposed to be cutting the lawns round Shadwell Court when he was caught by 'The Squire' chatting to one of the housemaids, after a previous warning. Instead of dismissal, Alf was sent in isolation to a large breck on the edge of the estate to pull 'canker weeds' and he was given a piece-work price to make sure he earned his money. However Alf had the last laugh. He almost doubled his weekly income which at that time was £1.5.0 and he also earned the local title of 'The Canker King' and was soon reinstated to his former job. When 'The Squire' passed on, Alf was left a legacy for good services, about £40, a small fortune then.

There was no more hired help when we were reckoned to be old enough to work. There were six boys and a girl in our family and all the boys had experience in thatching before and after leaving school.

It was unusual for us to receive wages so we were keen to find other jobs when another brother left school.

My first real memory of thatching goes back to 1912, when we had a disastrous harvest. Heavy rain for days caused tremendous flooding. Some crops were washed down the River Thet, corn stacks were soaked and looked like green mounds when the sodden grain grew all over them. Thatching straw which had been carted to stacks, or sites where stacks were intended, were heaps of 'muck'. It was serious for our family, indeed for lots of families, especially thatchers, who relied on the extra harvest money to pay rents and necessary clothes for the winter.

The Rector of Bridgham at that time, Rev. H. W. Blunt, whose grounds included riverside meadows, also had losses. Fowls, hen coops and many of his haycocks went down the river. He could not 'forgive and forget' even after the remnants of the battered crops had been brought in, and he refused to hold a Harvest Thanksgiving Service that year in spite of requests and criticisms in local pulpits and papers.

A poem composed by farm workers in Bridgham, including Albert Hubbard, Bert Whitrod and Bert Meek, was sent to press by Thomas Reeve (my father) who was then Sexton at Bridgham Church in October 1912:-

'After the Flood,' Bridgham, August 12, 1912

There's a little village by the river Thet
That have not had a Harvest Festival yet.
The Rector has given as the reason
This has been such a disastrous season.
The men have had to idle stand
While crops lie rotting on the land
Or what is enough to make one shiver
Are floating down the flooded river.
Now we all admit its been a bad season
But cannot think this is sufficient reason

15

For withholding our thanks for what we have got.
It might have been worse had it *all* gone to rot.
Although the quality is not very good
It is not *all* washed away in the flood.
Though it took a long while to gather together,
Most people have finished in spite of the weather,
But now it's completed there's still plenty of 'growls',
Which must be caused by the loss of those fowls.

During one of Rev. Blunt's grumbles about the lost hens, he got little consolation from his gardener, Amos Cutter, who remarked, 'You should have taken my advice, Sir, and kept ducks.'

The same 'poets' who wrote 'After the Flood' also wrote this verse on an elevator at a stack we thatched, much to the annoyance of the foreman ('masterman') Mr Jillings.

Bertie Whitrod does the stacking,
Carver does the binding
Jillings is the masterman
Who goes about fault-finding.

I will explain the 'Carver does the binding' line in the verse, because this job could be confused with the corn-cutting by binder mentioned on p.18.

During the corn-carting a gang of eight or ten men would operate. The stacker, who was usually the 'Harvest Lord', would be assisted by four men on the stack and one unloading the wagons. Three would alternate in pitching the sheaves off the loads into the elevator, or, prior to the introduction of these machines, they would pitch them on to a 'chair-hole'. This was a shelf left half way up the stack where one of the men stood to transfer them higher up the stack or across the other side. He was called the 'Bully' and the man nearest to him distributed the sheaves to the 'Stacker' and the 'Binder'. The former laid the outside courses which shaped the stack, and the Binder followed him round with inside courses placed half way on the outside sheaves to prevent them from slipping ('bind' them).

When the elevator came, the unloader and the Bully had a much easier job. Their sheaf-moving was either on the level or down hill. The poor old horse then had the monotonous job of walking round and round, drawing the pole turning the large cog-wheel which operated the connecting rod driving the elevator. Mentioning the horses, I think every true horse-lover was pleased when tractors took over the corn-cutting binders. This was a cruel job for the animals. To see them coupled up to the binder tow-pole was often heart-breaking. It usually required two men to lift the pole with the weight of the binder pressing heavily forward. (The machine was a little better balanced after the driver got seated at the back end.) The cross-bar would be strapped to the two inside horses' collars and this very often caused a raw patch on the horses' withers and the only relief they got was an extra piece of sack packing or an occasional change to outside horse which pulled by traces and whippletree, without having the weight of the pole. Two sets of three horses were used, and usually changed at two-hour intervals, but when a field was nearing the final acre or two, or rain threatened, the poor old horses would be forced along to the end by a long whip or a boy riding the inside horse. I have seen them leave the field dripping with sweat, foam and blood.

Amid all the heartaches of 1912 my brother Tom and I, who were too young to know the seriousness of the losses, were secretly delighted because Father was unable to thatch for days on end, and we were able to lie in bed, listening to the thunderous roar of the water trying to get through West Harling bridge. Tom had not left school and I was only ten, and if the weather had been suitable we would have been out at 5 a.m., or earlier if we had a longer journey. At that age we surely did not enjoy the work. Our job was 'pulling straw.' This entailed turning the straw off the cart, spreading water over every few 'forkfuls', and shaking into a 'bed'. The straw would then be pulled by handfuls into a row and 'yelmed'. This meant straightening out the straw and striking out most of the short pieces. The 'yelms' would be wide enough to cover a 'course' up the stack roof and the quantity of yelms depended on the length of the roof. Five to seven were the usual numbers and these were put in 'frails' (or yokes) to keep them flat and together, for carrying up the ladder. Father could really lay it on and we would soon be told off if we kept him waiting after he called 'shoof'.

It was during the making up of the bunches which required the odd numbers of yelms when we sometimes got into trouble. We alternated in pulling the extra yelm, but if there was some distraction we would forget who was due to make the odd one. An argument would follow, sometimes a tussle which would be ended by father coming down the ladder and threatening to 'lay a brotch across our backsides.'

The work was hard and our fingers got very sore, mainly because the straw often included a quantity of sharp thistles and there were no rubber gloves in those days.

We thought it a great treat to have a 'binder' cutting corn in a field nearby where we were at work. Father would 'let us off' when the corn cutting was nearing the last acre or two, so that we could help to catch the rabbits and be given one or two in the share-out afterwards. This was an assurance of a good hot dinner or supper during the next days. Rabbit pie or stew was a great dish.

Writing of the cooked rabbits reminds me of the wonderful share-out which happened during this meal, when each of us knew the 'joint' we would receive without any choice or argument. I cannot remember all the allowance, but I know father had the head, neck and liver, brother Tom had the back joint with the trunk attached which grandmother Reeve called the 'skep', and I always received the back

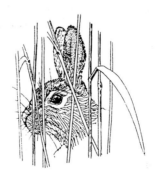

18

portion with the kidneys still joined. We all had a light dumpling (or 'Norfolk Swimmer') and plenty of vegetables. If we were lucky enough to have a small piece of pork cooked with the rabbit this had to be saved for another day.

Mother always brought a hot dinner or 'fourses' to the harvest fields if we were working within a mile or two of home. We always enjoyed these 'spreads' in the straw near the corn stacks, and we looked forward to her coming with the milk-cans containing the hot food hung on various parts of a pram. Mother was also good at making home-brewed beer. God knows how she found the time. There were often six of us sitting under the stack for these harvest meals.

If the harvest was a fairly good one, Tom and I, who were in the Church Choir, would be given about 2/- for the Choir's annual outing to Yarmouth - our only payment. These outings were always given free by the Rev. Blunt, even in the 'disastrous year.'

We moved from stack to stack or to different farms by pony and cart, and it was an accident during one of these journeys that robbed us of a lot of rest. Father was driving on the Turnpike (now the A.11) which was very rough in those days before the tarred surfaces. Two of my brothers were also in the cart, and as usual were tired and had dropped off to sleep. Father must also have dropped off, although he never admitted it. The pony stumbled and fell, throwing all three passengers over his head on to the flint-covered road. They were not hurt badly, but were bruised and grazed. The worst casualty was the pony. He suffered severely cut knees which kept him out of action for a long time, and of course dropped his value. One of the first places a horse dealer looks at is the knees, which are examined for scars.

We had long walks to work after this, and Father managed on a borrowed bike. Anyway we were never allowed to fall asleep in a cart again.

Tom left school at 13 and worked with Father in 1914. They took on their first job away from home. We never heard much about their experiences, but the brothers left at home got to know Tom was terribly homesick, and he was not allowed to forget it, by us, for a long time after he returned home.

Copy of the estimate for the job:-

June 1914   Viscount Chetwynd
                   Wyndthorpe, nr Doncaster, Yorks
Thomas Reeve, Bridgham, Norfolk.   £   s.   d.

Reed thatching Dairy
          including Tarred rope and Binders   8. 11. 6
          18 feet ridge @ 1/3 including Brotches   1.   2. 6
          Cost of Reeds. 200 fathoms   16.   0. 0
          Rail fare for self and boy   2.   3. 4
                                                 _____
                                       Pd   27. 17. 4

Father made thousands of brotches every year, and during our school holidays and on Saturdays it was our job to cut the hazelwood into the required lengths and cut out some of the knots and bent sections. This job was usually done for the West Harling and Shadwell Estates. The accounts shown earlier proved this was not a very highly paid job. The finished brotches were sold for 10d per bundle. The last I bought were 14/-.

Money for some jobs was sometimes slow coming in. On several occasions an expected 'settlement' had not arrived when Father got home from work on Saturday evening, and I remember him driving to Croxton and Thetford to collect his dues. No wonder we could not be paid.

During one of these delays in settling for his work Dad and Mum had a very worrying time. He could not get his money and in consequence the shopkeeper could not be paid. I remember Father thatching some cottages in Kings Street, East Harling for the late Mr John Warby who was our grocer etc. When the thatching was finished there was only a few shillings to draw, the rest had to be left to square off an accumulated debt.

We all had to do our little bits. One very good job came in for myself and one brother and four other schoolboys. We were required to pick stones off the paddocks and brecks where the brood mares etc.

would be turned out in the Spring. This was a holiday or Saturday job and we were paid 1/- each per day, double the rate for boys then working on farms, and we picked up several much needed shillings. Another bonus was the handing in of any young rabbits, or the reporting of an occupied rabbit-hole. No rabbits were allowed on these paddocks because of the danger to the thoroughbred horses' feet. Later the 'gang' got split up and given an area each because we were caught larking about, and I am sure that after the split many of the rabbits handed in for 'bonus' were found far away from the paddocks.

Cattle-droving was another way we picked up a few pence and sometimes shillings. We had a bumper time during the various sheep or lamb sales at Harling which at one time attracted 25,000 sheep and lambs from farmers miles around. Flock after flock would be drove through Bridgham, some of them only about 100 yards apart, and the drovers and shepherds were glad of our assistance to prevent the animals from breaking into the village gardens or fields. In the evenings when the flocks would be going the opposite way, sometimes with the same drovers but new owners, we would meet them outside the village again, but our jobs varied a little at this time of the day. Flocks would be halted near the old 'Bridgham Lion' Inn and we were put two or three boys between each flock to prevent them mixing, and the eldest of us then benefitted from our experiences of other sales.

We ask for our money before the drovers etc. went in the pub because we had found many of them had spent out on beer when they came to resume their journey. One old shepherd named Cooper was certain to be 'skint' so we made certain to collect off him. Another named Ladell had no difficulty in getting help, he paid up alright and we often continued to 'drove' with him to Kilverstone, I think he went on to Croxton.

When we arrived home at night we would proudly turn out our pockets and hand over our earnings, and perhaps have a few coppers returned.

Before we leave the old shepherds I must mention the method used by the older ones in counting the sheep by the score. We youngsters thought it some gibberish to amuse or confuse us but I have learned this method was regular in use at the Harling Lamb Sales, Norfolk, as recently as 1890. I obtained the evidence from Miss Dora Smith of South Creake whose grandfather, George Bannel Smith was one of these grand old men. He died at Roydon near King's Lynn in 1920 and supplied this copy for us.

Yan,	Tan,	Tethera,	Pethera,	Pimp,	Sethera,
1	2	3	4	5	6

Lethera,	Hovera,	Covera,	Dik,	Yan-a-dik,
7	8	9	10	11

Tan-a-dik,	Tethera-dik,	Pethera-dik,	Bumpit,	Yan-a-bumpit,
12	13	14	15	16

Tan-a-bumpit,	Tethera-bumpit,	Pethera-bumpit,	Figgit.
17	18	19	20

8. Brettenham Barn, Shadwell, 1920 (now demolished)

Our pony had the 'gripes' one morning while we were repairing reed thatch on Thetford Abbey Farm buildings, and a donkey (my grandfather called them 'Jerusalem Cuckoos') was borrowed from Gus Cutter the Bridgham Blacksmith. Father hired a bike and brothers Peter and Walter rode in the donkey cart, but it took them hours to make the journey to Thetford, because they could not persuade 'Jenny' to get out of a walk. Yet on the homeward journey they were hardly in the cart before she went at full gallop and arrived home in good time. Next morning they found a remedy for Jenny's slow progress on the outward trip - just a couple of jabs on her backside with a sharpened brotch and they were 'full speed ahead.'

Thetford Warren Lodge had the most difficult roof which we kept in repair. Nowadays it would be scaffolded, but we managed with a 52 stave ladder which just reached the eaves, where we attached another ladder to work on the roof. We shed no tears when the Lodge was burned down some years later.

Other buildings which have recently disappeared through the march

9. Thetford Warren Lodge - only the central block of this large building now remains. The Warren was used for hunting parties by monarchs and Dukes of Norfolk from medieval to Stuart days

of progress at Thetford are the Cannons Lodge and Cannons Barn. We repaired the thatch on the barn during several different occupations. In the first world war it was used by troops, and later it was 'a tobacco drying depot. The tobacco plants were grown on the Croxton Estate in large quantities.

Mill Farm Cottage was another on our list which we worked on, and which is now demolished. The 'New Plover' stands near the site of the old cottage.

I remember George Clark, for whom we first thatched stacks at Waterloo Farm, Stanford, now in the Battle Area. He was badly in need of a thatcher when he persuaded Dad to take on his stacks. It was a long journey for pony and cart or bikes, but he paid 2d per yard more than our local farmers. We left home before dawn and it was bed time when we arrived home. Fortunately Mr Clark was what Father called an 'early farmer' who usually had his stacks built a week or so earlier than our 'afternoon' farmers nearer home.

There was always a good supply of beer, and every day he visited us in his pony cart with the order, 'Send the boy up to the house for the beer, Tom.'

For us boys, our greatest satisfaction came at the end of harvest, when we each received half-a-crown for 'shutting the water cart lids to prevent his turkeys getting into the tanks.'

Mr Clark later farmed at Thetford and Hargham, where we continued to do his thatching, and he always paid the 2d per yard extra. I carried on with the harvest thatching for his son for several years, later on.

Fred Nunn was a farm steward at Roudham Hall Farm, who always impressed us with his 'tall stories.' He was a well built man and tremendously strong. He could pick up a comb of wheat (18 stones) and set it on a waggon, and he often moved our 40 stave ladder, if there was no horse and waggon or cart nearby, carrying it on his shoulder and riding his sturdy bike, to a stack sometimes a mile away from the one we had finished.

Few people had daily papers in those days, but Fred Nunn collected one every day from Harling Road Station. There were one or two rather illiterate lads on the farm who would ask about the news. Sometimes they would hear some fantastic stories, supposed to be in the papers, which Fred read out to them, but knowing his reputation, after getting 'caught' a few times, they were careful about repeating them.

Tom and I joined the West Harling Troop Boy Scouts in 1913 and I never regretted the courses we took to qualify for various badges and the discipline we learned to accept. Yet looking back there were occasions which seem ridiculous.

There was the time when Mum had a disagreement with the Bridgham Rector, Rev. Blunt, because we attended morning Sunday School at the Wesleyan Chapel while we belonged to the Church Choir and the afternoon Sunday School. Mum kept us away from Church Sunday School and we attended Church Service in the afternoons at West Harling Church with a party of other boy scouts from Bridgham. I well remember the ritual observed at these services. Everyone had to be in Church before Sir Edmund and Lady Nugent, and when the doors opened for them the whole congregation had to stand and face the aisle.

This was how our change back to Bridgham Church came about. Some of our 'gang' were late arrivals at a service and we hustled quickly to our seats, but not without disaster. Most of us wore hob-nailed boots, which had to be cleaned up for Sundays after being worn every day, and these made an awful clatter on the iron gratings down the centre aisle, added to by one of our members skidding and crashing down. Next day our Scout Master Miss Violet Nugent came to Bridgham and made peace between the parties, and we had no afternoon services at West Harling except when there were Scout parades.

We had some good times scouting, at camps, rallies, and a good party at Sir Edmund and Lady Nugent's Golden Wedding celebrations, but the smaller things, which thank goodness did not find a way into the Scout records, seem better remembered. We had a long walk home and on the way home across West Harling Common we visited most of the ponds to find water hen and other water fowl nests, from which

25

we usually took the eggs to provide us with luxurious custards and fried breakfasts. We knew the art of missing the keepers. Later in the year our haversacks would be stuffed with mushrooms, then walnuts, chestnuts and hazelnuts from the woods which we had to pass through.

No doubt we should have been punished if we had been reported, because this estate was ruled with a certain tyranny which was exercised against people who overstepped the line - for example, if a girl 'got into trouble' her parents were automatically forced to leave the house and the estate. Girl servants had to dress in black, attend church at least once a day, and their 'boy friends' had to be approved.

3. The First World War and After

During the 1914 war we took our turn as orderlies at the West Harling Racquet Court Hospital.

The first batch of four wounded soldiers came straight from the trenches in France, caked in mud up to their armpits. Indeed it was one of my jobs to help scrape the mud off their clothes. I kept some of the mud in a tin labelled 'Flanders Mud' for years.

Another duty was collecting the suppers from the kitchen at West Harling Hall for the patients and nursing staff. We also had to take the 'left-overs' and containers back to the Hall. During this time we hoped and longed for something to eat but we were rarely given anything. The exceptions came when Mrs Coote was on duty. She was a gamekeeper's wife and she knew something about hungry boys. She would set us out a good plateful before our walk home through the lonely old woods. We always hoped her turn of duty would coincide with ours. When it did not, we were supposed to carry the 'left-overs' and containers back in boxes *untouched,* but I am afraid our half-starved tummies got the better of our Scouts' Honour on several occasions.

It was quite a walk from the Racquet Court (now demolished) to the Hall and we were sometimes waylaid by other off-duty members of our Troop, including the coachman's sons who would hide in the box bushes until we went back with the food.

Another offence which we innocently carried out was when the soldiers were convalescent. There was no pub in West Harling and we were asked to bring one or two bottles of beer from Bridgham to the soldiers who would meet us in the woods, and no doubt our good turns were appreciated by them, but we later learned this was 'out of order.' Thank goodness the offence never reached our Scout Master.

I left school when I was 12 years old by a 'Shortage of Labour Certificate', granted to pupils who had reached a fair standard of education (for those days) and with an application from a farmer who had lost his men for war service. Mr A. W. Farr, Grove Farm,

Bridgham, was my applicant. This was in late 1914 and I was promised 3/- per week, but I was considered a good worker during my first few days and my wages increased to 3/6 on the first pay night. I was thrilled to work on a farm because I thought this would mean no 'straw pulling', but I was soon disillusioned. I was borrowed to do the job occasionally and I was glad to get back after an incident on the farm.

I was 'horse-raking' between the corn shocks on a 100 acre breck when a terrible thunderstorm blew up. I was inexperienced with horses and I always feared thunderstorms when a kid. There were no workmates or shelter near. I was scared and the horse was even worse. I had no coat or shelter and I had to stand holding the plunging and rearing horse to stop him running away with the rake. I was unable to get him out of the shafts. Anyway when the next thunderstorm came a few days later I had the shelter of a corn stack and the company of my dad.

When the war finished the younger farm workers like myself had to make way for the ex-service men who were lucky enough to be returned. I went to help in thatching the roofs which had got in bad repair during the war years. Tom had been working on Harling Aerodrome during the last years of the war and Father had Walter, after he left school, to help him. Father's work included trussing hay for Army horses and thatching shelters for German Prisoners of War on Thetford Warren Camp.

It was 1920 before I was allowed to do any actual thatching. Father was very cautious about our qualifications. We were always referred to as 'boys' even after we were married. He would inspect a roof for repairs and tell the owners he was sending two of his 'boys' to do the job. Some of them got a surprise when we turned up. Perhaps they expected to see boys in 'knicker-bockers' come to do the work.

Village life revived in 1919-20. Quoit Clubs, which existed in nearly every village, re-formed. Bridgham 'Lion' was one of the strongest in the district, in spite of losing some of their best players in the war, including Albert Hubbard, Ernie (Miles) Meek, Will Rudland and George Holmes. Other outstanding clubs were Old Buckenham

Crown, Thetford Abbey, and Barnham. All clubs had their headquarters at a public house where a splendid social evening was held after the match. The Reeve brothers played an active part in the sport for Bridgham 'Lion.'

We also helped to reorganise local football, and formed a club in Bridgham for the first time. During some of our matches there were four Nicholsons, four Reeves and three Holmes in the Bridgham team. Later I went with Alan Nicholson to play for Thetford Town, then in the Norfolk & Suffolk League, and we both got recognition by Norfolk County.

As a goalkeeper I found my long reach a great asset, and this had advantages for me in my thatching. The extra inches often spared a ladder being moved or another added at the top.

After thatching some farm buildings and cottages with Father at Great Barton, I did my first complete thatching harvest and I learned another lesson here. The stacks were hurriedly stacked and I was keen to get them thatched as soon as the roofs were finished. Most of them developed a lean after they had settled, leaving a steep pitch on one side and a nearly flat one on the other. This usually happened after a few days and by that time I had thatched them in. When the rains came the thatch on the flat side was far from waterproof and Father received a letter complaining about the wet corn which I did my best to explain. Anyway this never happened again with my thatching because any stacks that did not satisfy me had to be 'right sided' before I covered them in.

Next time I thatched stacks it was at West Rudham and I must have done the job properly because the following year I received a letter which I proudly showed to Father. This requested me 'to do the thatching again this year, because we know you will do them well.'

I did not have to look around for 'thatching harvests' after that.

*****

I made another break from thatching in the mid twenties. I worked on a Land Reclamation Scheme, building a sea bank on Wingland Marsh, Terrington St Clement, for Mornement and Ray, a firm of

Steam Engine Contractors, East Harling.

I started as a baulkman's mate. Baulks were the scoops which were pulled between two steam engines to get soil up to the new bank. I graduated to relief driver before I left.

We lived in quarters similar to an army camp, which I suppose was appropriate - our boss was a Colonel. One night an exceptional and surprise high tide broke through a temporary barrage in a creek, one of the last gaps remaining to be filled in the bank. It was called Johnson's Creek. We had spent several days assembling materials, huge timbers, wooden 'rafts' (platforms for the engines) and other valuable equipment, and these were soon swept out of position. While the tide was coming in everything looked recoverable but on the ebb hundreds of timbers etc. were in danger of being taken out to sea through the gap.

10. Land Reclamation at Wingland in 1926 - a Burrell Steam Engine during a High Tide

30

Mr Bob Hatton, the manager, came into our sleeping quarters and called for six volunteers to go out salvaging and tethering as much as possible. He also said he preferred swimmers and some of us were glad we were.

I was one of the volunteers who went out on this miserably cold night and returned three hours later, soaked to the skin, but pleased to think we had saved hundreds of pounds worth of equipment. When we drew our pay on the Friday night we received our reward, an extra 2/6 and a letter of thanks from the firm. This caused quite a laugh among our mates who had kept snugly in their bunks.

Many of us cycled home the 45 miles each way on Saturday afternoons, returning Sunday nights.

After 'wintering and summering' this job, I returned to thatching again, had a good harvest at West Rudham and came home with £14 in my pocket, a good sum in those days towards 'setting up a house.' I was courting then.

I thatched some buildings at Thorpe Farm, West Harling (now demolished), then tried another job lorry-driving. My brother Walter was already driving, after a spell of railway work which finished when he was posted to Manchester.

I learned to drive on a 1914-18 war-time 'Riker' which was on solid tyres and fitted with carbide gas lamps, oil side and tail lamps. These vehicles had leather-bound clutches which, until they were worn a bit smooth, would cause the front wheels to rear up when starting a heavy load. Brakes were also unreliable.

We often worked 80 to 90 hours a week during the sugar beet season, but much of this time was spent waiting to get unloaded at the factories. We kept in touch with thatching by carting thatching materials and getting a few weeks off to thatch stacks at harvest time. Tom had finished with thatching and worked with tractors. Later he became a fitter and remained in that trade.

1927 was remembered because of another wet harvest. We finished our last stack on October 5th.

Here is a copy of the accounts.

11. At Martham Station, 1928 - B. S. Reeve and the Riker Lorry

Mr E. A. Rowell, West Rudham Hall, King's Lynn
(2 men)Thatching 40 corn and hay stacks

423 yds @ 1/8 per yd	£35. 5. 0.
Received on a/c	21. 0. 0.
Paid Oct 5/27	14. 5. 0.

Mr B. Butcher, W. Rudham
(2 men) 8 stacks   88 yds at 1/8   £7. 11. 8.
                             Paid Oct 5/27

      1928 was fine throughout the harvest and we finished about the same amount of thatching for these farmers on September 13th.

Hay trussing was also allied to the thatching trade and we often took on this job during the slack periods of our Transport days. I think this was the hardest earned money of all. I used a large cutting knife and with other necessary tools it was a struggle to carry the tools on a bike. The pay was 6/- per ton (40 trusses to the ton) and to cut 2 tons per day was considered a very good day. If the lorries or waggons came for the trusses while I was working at the stack I would be paid another 6d per ton. This worked out about seven trusses for 1s.

Another seasonable job was reed-cutting. This began in January and fitted in nicely after the sugar beet factories had closed and many lorries 'stood up'. My brothers and I very often cut reeds while other unfortunate drivers had to go on the dole. We cut the reeds which grew on Larling, Snetterton, and Shropham Fens. Father paid the tenants or the Parish Councils for the 'standing crop' and we cut as

12. Cutting Reed at Shropham Fen, - J. Reeve (left) and B. Reeve.

much as possible. There was a knack in getting across the deep water and the almost bottomless spring-holes. We found it better to proceed slowly and make sure to bend the reed stubble over to form a foothold. We were almost sure to break through if we put our feet straight down, especially when carrying a load of 10 bunches tied up with a rope on our backs, and this was the only method we had for getting them to higher ground.

We had other lads to help us occasionally and this was when we found how much our experience helped. There was Jack Waller who would try very hard to follow our footsteps across these treacherous spots but he still broke through a few times a day. Indeed he was so regular at taking a 'dip', he not only brought spare socks, he also brought trousers and shirt. This would have been fun during summer time but it was very uncomfortable in January and February.

There were no such luxuries as long rubber boots when we cut our first reeds. We used leather boots which just came over our knees, and we borrowed these from Mornement & Ray, Steam Contractors, East Harling. When these had been worn by other workers in water and stored away the leg parts would be wrinkled and very hard. After being moulded to other legs these creases were terribly uncomfortable for our limbs. We had to walk almost stiff-legged and this was difficult in the worst places. It was necessary to heat mutton fat or other grease to rub into these creases and joints before starting in the water, partly to help soften the leather and also to help make them water-tight.

In 1919-20 Father sold thousands of bunches of reed for paper pulp making. We cut these from Larling and Snetterton fens and this helped to clear up several acres which had not been previously cut, because the reeds required for paper did not need to be of such high quality as for thatching.

We reckoned to cut about 12,000 bunches (2,000 fathoms). A fathom is 6 bunches, each a foot in diameter. In later years the reeds were useless on these fens. Deep draining of the nearby River Thet lowered the water level on the reed beds and encouraged bushes and other growth to smother the reeds.

After cutting, the reeds were dressed. This means cleaning out weeds and short pieces, then bumping the bottom ends on a board to level them out before being stacked and thatched.

There was still a lot of hard work to be done when the reeds were required for thatching because lorries were unable to get near our stacks on the soft fen land, so once again we had to carry them to a site nearer the road.

We preferred reap-hooks for cutting our reeds. Scythes were often used, but we could cut and carry out 100 bunches each per day and we felt satisfied with our method. Nowadays the cutting is mainly mechanised.

When the weather got too bad or the water too high, we had other materials to get prepared on drier ground - the brotches and rods used on ridges and in straw thatching, and the hazel binders (or sways) used for binding on the reeds.

*****

Having these connections with thatching I was proud to think I had never drawn a penny from the dole, but in 1930 I nearly broke that record. Work with transport was slack as usual and at the end of my first week of married life I 'got my cards' (not a very good wedding present). When the reed-cutting etc. was finished I went to 'sign on' at Thetford, but on the way I heard of an 'odd man's' job on the Shadwell Estate for Captain Birkin - he later became Sir Henry Birkin, but was better known as 'Tim', one of the great Bentley racing drivers. He was the 'shooting tenant', and world famous racing drivers Woolf Barnate, Klen Kitson and Beris Harcourt-Woods were frequent visitors and all great shots. Tim often joined in our local football and gathered together a team for charity games at Thetford during the Christmas holidays he spent at Shadwell. Titled men, well known sportsmen, keepers and odd men all joined in the 'frolics' after the game.

My job was helping to grow food and attractions for pheasants, looking after wild duck and a large variety of gun dogs, but to keep in touch with the old trade my brother and I made reed shelters for duck-shooting, reed thatched a boat house, and left for a few weeks on the harvest thatching.

I stayed for nearly two years working for 'Tim', but 1931 was a depressing year in many ways. Our family had grown up, some were married and only the youngest, Leslie, was at school. Mother was then able to have more leisure and more money to use, and no-one ever deserved it more. Then, after a sudden illness, she died unexpectedly in Norwich Hospital at the age of 52. Father was thatching in Surrey and arrived at the Hospital just before she died. How thankful we all were there was one girl in the family, Enid, who took over in her early teens. She looked after Les and kept a good home for Father for the rest of his life.

1932 was a bad year, for agriculture in particular, and we had to accept a 2d per yard reduction for stack thatching. This amounted to about £10 less, quite a loss in those days when the harvests were also getting smaller.

Dr G. S. Keeler's house in Connaught Road, Attleborough, which we thatched in 1933, is mentioned because it shows the variety in designs we used in our ornamental ridging. This one we called 'scalloped' and it took rather more time and materials than our usual patterns which we called 'diamond.' In later years when time became more valuable we always cut 'diamond' patterns unless otherwise requested. The estimate etc. shows the house was thatched in reed by Father and John on the front roof only. The back roof had been thatched with straw earlier.

Copy of estimate:-

Dr G. S. Keeler, Connaught Rd, Attleborough
Dec. 1932   Thomas Reeve & Son

15 squares reed thatching including reeds = £48.	0.	9
76 ft ridge @ 2/- including brotches	7.	12.	0
Hooks, rope and binders	3.	5.	0
Straw for ridge	2.	10.	0
Repairing south side	1.	12.	6
Pd -1933	63.	0.	3

13. Connaught Road, Attleborough, 1933

Also in 1933 I thatched a meadow hay-stack in Harling and the cost including brotches was 9/-. The owner gave me a 10/- note but I had no change. He later sent his gardener to my home to collect the 'bob'. 'Good old days'?

4. Norfolk and Beyond - from the 1930s to the 1950s

John was working with Father on several jobs in the Bognor Regis area in the 1930s. One of these houses was the home of Chesney Allen of the 'Crazy Gang' fame.

In 1936 they were overwhelmed with orders, and Walter and I were 'borrowed' from lorry-driving to help out. Walter worked with John on a house at Woodford, Cheshire, and Father and I thatched a new house and garage at Felpham in the Bognor area. I remember our job there because it was the only time we had to strip off our new thatch and start again. We commenced thatching within a short time of unloading our materials, with which we had travelled from Norfolk, well pleased because the builders had left the scaffolding intact, and we made good progress fixing the eave courses round the house. Imagine our dismay when the owner came and wanted a further overhang at the eaves which required an extension on the feet of the rafters. Plans were amended and we had to strip off our well tightened thatch to enable the carpenters to make the alterations. We also had to send home for 300 extra bunches of reeds because of the added length to the roof. Anyway we got paid for the extras.

This was my last thatching job till 1946, but Father and John were now joined by Leslie, the youngest of the family. He started work on a farm but decided to take up thatching in 1936 when Walter and I went back to our lorry-driving. That was Walter's last experience in thatching. He stayed in transport until he retired.

Father made many friends during his long thatching life and his travels to various parts of the country, but he had at least two bad customers. One in the south of England went bankrupt and paid out 1/3 in the pound. Another, in Cheshire, sold his house after having it thatched and emigrated without paying a penny for the thatching. These were severe blows in the 1930's. His greatest disappointment concerning his work came a few years earlier. He reed thatched a bungalow standing on the riverside at East Harling in 1925 and he had included special ornamentations all over the roof to the delight of the owner, Mr Fred Tillot. About six months later Father and I were straw thatching at Great Barton, Bury St Edmunds, and we were in lodgings. We went out in the evening for a drink and during our walk we saw a red glow in the sky towards home, and this held our interest for some time. Next morning we got the message which upset Father for a few days, 'Tillot's bungalow was burnt down.' The bungalow was replaced but never thatched again; only the surviving boathouse and other garden shelters remained to show traces of Father's skill.

Roudham Hall Farm barn was thatched with straw by Father, John and Les during 1936. It was stripped to the rafters. This was unusual, when straw thatching we tried to leave on some of the 'under coats'. This stripping was done because the roof was infested with rats, and when the rafters were cleared, wire netting was fixed to prevent rats returning by the inside route. Netting was also placed on the outside and the roof was bird and rat-proof for many years. This was probably the last complete straw thatch for this huge roof. It was the longest barn we worked on, 150 feet ridge, and the whole roof measured 70 squares. They used three large straw stacks on the roof.

Another beautifully timbered barn, where three generations of our family have worked, was at Knettishall Farm. This measured 106 feet long, 125 feet ridging including a front porch and was reed thatched. All my brothers have worked on this roof, but there is no record of a complete new thatch. We always renewed the thatch in sections. The barn was demolished in 1972.

*****

From 1936 lorry drivers were in greater demand, aerodromes etc. were being built, and the pay was better than in thatching, so at the start of the 1939 war I was in a 'reserved occupation.' Perhaps this turned out for the best. Brothers John and Les, not considered on essential work, had to join the army.

Les had an adventurous and sometimes bad time in the Far East, and John was wounded after the Normandy landings. He later went to

Palestine.

My war time driving experiences, which involved me in the London Blitz and various other raids, 'blackout' driving and 'hush hush' jobs, would fill several pages.

When war broke out our lorry head-lamps were fitted with masks which allowed only three hooded slits of light to show. These were improved after a number of accidents but were still very restricted. There were some happenings and regulations which were hard to understand.

A runway on Snetterton Airfield, from which the American C Squadron Fortresses operated, was damaged, and I was given an emergency order to fetch 15 tons of special quick-setting cement, I think it was called 'Aquacrete', from cement works in Kent, by the Thames. I set off from East Harling at 3 a.m. and made good time with the traffic light at that early hour. However, going down Dagenham Way, I was stopped by 'speed cops'. My emergency order which I produced had no influence on them, and I was duly summoned for exceeding the speed allowed and fined £2 at Stratford. So much for emergencies.

Another 'urgent' trip which turned out a farce was an order to pick up a 'Block Buster' bomb weighing about 10 tons at Marham Aerodrome one Saturday afternoon, to move to Mildenhall. After being loaded by a large crane, and provided with escort vans front and behind, we arrived at Mildenhall to find all crane-drivers missing from the camp. A long delay followed before a Flying Officer volunteered to 'have a go' with the crane. Some damage was done to the side of my lorry but it was eventually safely landed on wooden pads, but I was watching with some concern from behind a bomb bay bank some distance away.

*****

John and Les returned safely from the war in 1946. Les teamed up with father, and my last lorry load of reeds I delivered to them at Broad Walk, Prestbury, Cheshire. The owner was a former R.A.F.

Officer and a test pilot at A.V. Roe Woodford Aerodrome.

I finished with transport for good, and partnered John mainly on local houses and buildings neglected or damaged during the war. Reed thatching Coney Weston Post Office was our first job, then straw thatching Coney Weston Hall Farm House.

I was stripping the rotten thatch from a 'valley' when I disturbed a very strong wasps' nest. I made a hasty retreat down the ladder but received a few stings on the way down. It was 'wash day' for the lady of the house, and she offered me a pail of boiling soap suds from the copper to throw into the nest so that we could proceed with our thatching. I dashed up the ladder, threw the suds and expected the surplus water to run down the roof, but there was a hidden cavity under the thatch which allowed the water to go straight into the bedroom and below to a well kept room. Carpets and ceiling, also some of the furniture, looked a mess. It was some time before we were on good terms with the very 'house proud' lady.

I was better treated by those wasps than Les when he was stripping a house at Stygal in Cheshire. He pulled a complete nest out with the old thatch, and during his scramble down the ladder the whole lot fell on his head. His shirt was wide open, and he later counted over 40 stings on various parts of his body. He was shut in the front room of the cottage while he stripped and shook out all his clothes. Even after he dressed he was stung again by stray ones left in his trousers. He had a stiff drink of brandy from the owner of the house, but had no other treatment. A doctor who checked him up in the evening said he must have been in wonderfully fit condition.

The winter of 1946-47 was very severe, but it was some advantage to us during reed-cutting. We cut thousands of bunches on ice and the carrying out was much easier than plodding through three or four feet of water. Heavy flooding followed when the thaw came, but we had carried our reed to higher ground by then.

Father and Les were reed thatching Knutsford 'White Bear', Cheshire, during the coldest of the weather. It was bad enough for Les, but father was 72 years old then. He was tough, but we think this decided him to 'call it a day.' He retired from regular active thatching that year, and confined his thatching to local repairs and short spells with Les during the better weather. However, he was still the 'boss.' He bought our first van that year, a second-hand Austin Seven 5 cwt.

Severe gales also caused trouble in the spring of 1947 and we carried out major repairs in the neighbouring villages and in the Newmarket area. Sandwich Stud and Hascombe Stud buildings all received gale damage.

14. Hascombe Stud, Chevely, 1937

Hascombe Stud House which Father had originally reed thatched in 1937 seemed fated to be damaged. Before the paint was hardly dry, a plumber was called in to de-freeze the water pipes and while using a blow lamp in the 'false roof' he set light to the thatch, which was burnt off in a very short time, and Father had to return and thatch again.

It was while we were repairing the gale-damaged roofs in 1947 that John had a fall from his ladder and broke his thumb. He was taken to Cambridge Hospital where his hand was put in plaster. Even this did not prevent him working and he never stayed away from the job. The only part of the work he could not do was writhing (twisting) the brotches when we repaired the ridges. When the time came for the removal of the plaster it had worn through and fell apart.

Fortunately 1947 summer was very hot and we had most of the buildings repaired before there was much damage inside.

John and I went to Scarborough for two weeks repairing a gale-damaged house for Mr Cockerline. I think this was the only reed thatched house in Scarborough. Mr Cockerline was a race-horse owner and no doubt had heard of our work at Newmarket. This house was the only one we worked on with the roof forming a square and not thatched on the inside. It was built with the thatch showing all round the roof, but the centre, concealed by a thatched ridge, was covered in flat lead and bitumen with a lead gutter passing through the thatch to the outside. We found the flat lead roof very advantageous when we renewed the ridge.

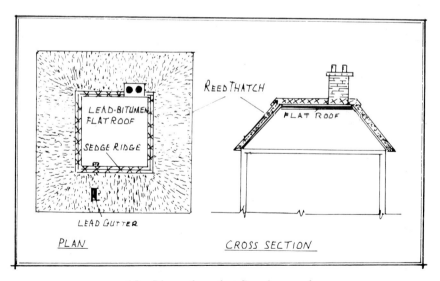

15. Plan of roof at Scarborough

43

We attended one of the matches during the Scarborough Cricket Festival. We were Len Hutton 'fans.' He confirmed all our admiration for him, but we were disappointed when he was caught out just short of another century.

Our landlady was a wonderful person, a widow over 70 years old and real Yorkshire. Our broad Norfolk dialect and her Yorkshire caused many a laugh when we met her family in a nearby pub.

We noticed she was saving kindling wood for the winter and we realised she could use the old broken brotches we pulled out of the thatch, and we brought her bundles home every day to store when we came from work on the local buses. One evening John had a neatly tied bundle under his arm and he was standing at the far end of the bus which stopped suddenly throwing John off balance. The string must have broken loose from his bundle because on the way to the back exit the brotches dropped everywhere leaving the centre gangway littered with hundreds of broken brotches. We often wondered what was said when the bus arrived back at the station. I am sure nobody there knew what they were.

Les married in 1947 and with his wife, who was a Manchester girl, settled in Longsight with plenty of thatching orders in hand. We (John and I) came back to local work, and a house we reed thatched in Kenninghall for Miss Fletcher in 1948 provided us with problems we only found in some very old roofs. The ceilings were plastered to the reed flaking (reeds laid across the rafters instead of battens). This added to the difficulty in finding the wood for binding on the new thatch. This was done by probing with a 'needle' and a miss with this tool very often meant piercing the ceiling. When the binding hooks were knocked into the rafters the plaster often cracked and dropped into the bedrooms. However, we warned Miss Fletcher this would happen and she was prepared for the trouble, but we had the job of clearing up the mess in the bedrooms at the end of each day of thatching.

Kenninghall Rectory Tithe Barn which was near to our last mentioned job we thatched in straw. This old building has now been pulled down.

44

It was quite a luxury to have our meals at home, but this was possible during our next job (1948), on our neighbour's cottage (Mr Webster - Mrs Boggan) which needed some repairs and a new ridge. We completed this before setting out on our travels again. This time we went to ridge a large house, 'Kingmere', Summery Lane, Felpham, Sussex, but while we were unloading our materials the occupier came out and warned us that no repairs would be done while he was in residence and he was staying there for three months. We contacted the owner and their solicitors who had overlooked a clause in the letting agreements which said 'the tenant will be left undisturbed during his tenancy.' Next day we left for home after being assured of our expenses.

I don't know who finally carried out the work - we did not go again.

*****

September 6, 1948 was a birthday for me, but remembered so well because this year it coincided with the official opening of our East Harling Memorial Playing Field, and I was responsible for getting together a Harling and District team to oppose a Norwich City XI for the opening match. The game proved a great attraction and gave the field a wonderful start. John and I had many years of pleasure helping with various clubs and functions there.

Les was now thatching on his own; Father visited him occasionally, sometimes travelling on the lorry carrying thatching materials from Norfolk. Knutsford, Holmes Chapel, and Plumbly, all in Cheshire, were places where Les had contracts.

We had our first local council contract in 1949. A block of Old Person's Homes at Euston for the Thingoe R.D.C., and we learned a lesson here. Our estimate was accepted by the council and we carried out the work and a few extras due to alterations in the roof including a thatched memorial plaque, to the satisfaction of the council. Then the architect decided it would assure a longer life for the straw ridges if we covered these with wire netting. This was not included in our estimate. We agreed with the architect this should be done, and acting

45

on his verbal order we fixed the netting and added the cost to our bill, but we were never paid for this extra because we could not produce an authorisation in writing from the council, and the £27.18.0 remains in the books unpaid. There was proof we had the netting, because at that time wire netting was on 'permit', and the Thingoe Council issued the permit for this particular netting. We tried to persuade father to have us tear the netting off again but he would not agree. Maybe he was right, the birds would have played havoc with our workmanship in a very short time.

We had problems binding the reed on this roof because the rafters were an unusual size for thatching, 6" x 1". Timber for these was also in short supply. Perhaps I should explain the method we used in fixing the reeds. After the reed bundles have been placed in position a 'binder' (hazel stick) is laid across and iron hooks are hammered into each rafter, which are 15 to 18 inches apart. By hammering the hooks in, the binder would tighten the reed. The thatch would then be a finished thickness of about 12 inches and the binders about 18 inches from the outside would be covered by the next course. The rafters, fixed edgeways, had only about an inch face in which to hammer our

16. Thingoe R.D.C. Bungalows, Euston 1949

hooks, which were made of quarter-inch steel rods, and the slightest deviation would mean splitting the rafters. In a very awkward spot one of us would go inside the roof and guide the point of the hook to its accurate position before hammering home.

It was during one of these manoeuvres when I was put in a nasty position. I was guiding the hook when, amidst the noise of the carpenters working inside, John mistook my replies to his probing through the thatch and he hammered the hook into the rafter via the middle of my thumb-nail. Luckily he was able to draw it out fairly quickly, but I had to have medical attention after first aid at a neighbouring cottage.

We straw thatched a row of eight cottages in Suffolk where we found all the tenants at loggerheads with one another. This did not handicap us in any way, indeed we benefitted. We were kept well supplied with refreshments all the way down the row, each occupier competing with the one whose roof we had just finished. It was amusing to watch them sweeping up our old thatch outside their doors, without much conversation, and not going an inch further than their own boundaries. However, I believe we helped to bring some of them together during our long stay there.

*****

When a Norfolk Thatchers Association was formed, we were among the first members. W. Farman, North Walsham, Fred and Vic Harvey, Salhouse, Harry Oakley from Acle and Walter Drake from Mundham were also active members. Father served as Hon. Secretary for several years. Work was plentiful and we were able to pass on jobs to fellow members. This assured the customers they would get a competent craftsman for their roofs.

We were concerned about the shrinking of our local reed crops about this time and we began to benefit from being members of the Association. We were introduced to other sources of supply and have since had a good allocation of first class reeds and sedge from the Norfolk Broads. (Sedge is used for ridging instead of straw.)

47

Reeds were extensively used for flaking over the rafters instead of battens, to give a tidy appearance from inside. Our grandfather and father used an intricate pattern for weaving the flaking, but this got 'lost' in our later estimates for economy reasons. It was one of our first jobs in thatching with Father, to strip off the old thatch and flake the roof. We laid the reeds across the rafters and bound them on with a small handful of reeds laid in line with the rafters. When reeds became scarcer in the locality this method was left out of our estimates and the roofs were battened closer, and in some cases 'under-felted.'

Harling Farm barn, on which we have done several repairs to the straw thatch may now have worn out its last coat of thatch. Modern grain storage and machinery have been installed and a more suitable roof may be added. It was a miracle this old barn survived when in 1945 a liberator loaded with petrol crashed in flames 30 yards from the barn roof and destroyed the adjoining cowsheds.

Twenty years later another fire, started in a piggery only 12 yards away, was kept under control to enable the old barn to escape again, while the nearby buildings were gutted.

The need for wire-netting straw thatch was proved when we included netting in our estimate for straw thatching Clay Hall Farm House, Blo Norton, and for economic reasons the netting items were refused. However, within a few weeks of the completion of the thatching, the roof was riddled with bird-holes and the owner had to have second thoughts after the damage had been done.

Some of our misfortunes may suggest thatching is a dangerous occupation, but our falls were mainly due to the disregard of conditions. In late 1949 we were repairing a fairly high roof near Thetford Golf Links, and a sharp frost at night made the 'staves' slippery. Instead of waiting for the thaw I got cracking on the roof and soon forgot about the icy foothold. When I reached sideways my feet slipped and I took a dive off the roof. Luckily I landed head first into a clipped hedge, and I received only a few facial scratches and bruises which kept me away from work only a few days.

Many years later I toppled off a farm-house at Banham Fen - again this was carelessness. The top stave of the ladder had been exposed to the weather during storage. This broke in my hand while I was moving the ladder at the top of the house. Fortunately I fell into a barley field, if I had fallen the other side I would have landed on concrete or other hard ground. I was taken to hospital and detained as a precaution, otherwise I would have been back at work in a day or two.

The amount of thatching we carried out can be judged by the places we worked. These included Thetford, Brandon, Mundford, Wretham, Kilverstone, Great Hockham, Great Ellingham, Attleborough, Old and New Buckenham, Banham, Barnham, Garboldisham, Market Weston, Coney Weston, Botesdale, Barningham, Hopton, Riddlesworth Estate, Diss and Rushford. The last named brings to mind the church mentioned in grandfather's account of 1866 and a notable entry in Father's diary for 1898 which showed that Father stripped and reed thatched this church roof, and in 1951 John and I did its first major repairs. We fixed a new straw ridge and did a few minor repairs to the reed thatch. We suggested renewing the wire netting but this was decided against. Twenty years later it was requiring further attention.

*****

In 1951 we found a welcome source of supplies of brotches from Percy and Stanley Coe, twin brothers in business as 'Wood Reeves and Hurdle Makers', of Burgate near Diss, and we remained customers of these very reliable people until they retired (the same year as myself, 1967).

Brotches, also called Broaches, Spars and Spits, are usually about 2 feet in length for house-thatching, and after sharpening at both ends they are trimmed to make them easier for writhing (twisting) in staple fashion to pin down the thatch or to straddle the rods (liggers) which are shown on the outside of the thatch as part of the ornamentations, and a guide for cutting the various patterns on the ridge. A good thatcher also trims the rods to take off the rough edges and form chisel ends under the twisted brotches at the joints. Many a wet day have

49

been spent sharpening brotches and it was a favourite joke of John's, when people watched him deftly pointing each brotch with three accurate strokes at each end, he would ask 'How many strokes does it need for a good sharp brotch?' and nine out of ten would answer 'Three', and of course the answer is 'None.'

Les's work in Cheshire consisted mainly of reed thatching but John and I found more straw thatching and there were supplies of wheat or rye straw in nearly every village, but in the 1950s straw began to get scarce. We overcame this problem for a few years by buying whole stacks of straw and carting the necessary quantity to the jobs sometimes 20 miles from the stack. When combine harvesters got established we obtained our straw only from a few sympathetic farmers who threshed by 'drum' especially for the thatching straw.

In 1952 we reed thatched the last remaining thatched cottage in Bridgham (Manor Cottage). It is sad to think there may soon be no evidence of Reeves' thatching in their home village. In 1912 there were ten cottages, two barns and many other buildings. Even our pony's stable was reed thatched. Records show the Church was thatched in 1800.

During 1952 we reed thatched a reconstructed cottage named 'Frogs' Bottom', Raspberry Vale, Boughton, near Canterbury. I mention this because this was the only job the four of us, Father, John, Leslie and I worked on at the same time.

We started on July 3rd and our aim was to finish before August Bank Holiday (then the first week in August). Father had retired from actual thatching; he was 77 then but he came for the last week, and Les broke off a job in Cheshire for a fortnight to help us. We worked hard and we finished on schedule. It was a difficult roof to get round. There were thirteen windows in the thatch; some were so close together we could not get a ladder between them. There was also a front porch to thatch, but we all had a marvellous time while we were there.

Mr and Mrs R. Jenkins, the owners, lived on the site in a caravan. They fed us well and took us back and forth to our lodgings in Boughton. They also took us on visits to the Kent coast towns and to

17a. Frog's Bottom, Boughton, Kent, - work in progress

17b. Frog's Bottom - work completed.

51

see many of their friends. Most of these 'off duty' periods were at week ends. At other times it was hard work and long hours. It was during the cherry-picking season and the cottage was surrounded by cherry orchards. It was here we had our first taste of cherry pie. I can recommend these.

John and I came back to more local work. We thatched in Denmark Street, Diss, and repaired Thetford Grammar School Pavilion before starting another season reed-cutting. Larling Fen and Shropham did not produce enough for our requirements and we cut on other fens at Garboldisham and Blo Norton, leaving our Broads allocation for supplying Les direct.

We bought a new van for the first time in 1953, a Ford 5 cwt. After using second-hand vehicles we found a new van a luxury. Les also had a better van at this stage.

In the spring we reed thatched the north side of the chancel end of Old Buckenham church, the south side had been thatched some years earlier but was in good condition.

Some of the cottages we thatched at Wretham in 1954 were mentioned in Peter Reeve's records in the 1860s. One was described as the 'Four Dweller on the Park', and another was Dunford 'Dubble' Cottages. We did not work on 'Barrick' Cottages, this had been demolished.

In 1955 we had our highest priced job, over £400, in the summer, reed-thatching the new 'Cock Inn' at Lavenham, built behind the old 'Cock' which was pulled down after its successor was completed. Father was still fairly active and would occasionally spend a day with ·us, and he continued to keep the books in order.

This job was made easier for us because the scaffold was left in position until we finished after eight weeks work. We were visited every week by the brewery officials who admired and complimented us on our progress, but never left us a free drink at the old 'Cock' during our time there. However, when the new premises were opened we were invited to a rather lavish official opening. We would have preferred the odd 'free pint' while we were working in the hot sun.

Mentioning the Lavenham 'Cock' reminded me of many other pubs

52

18. The Cock Inn, Lavenham, built and reed thatched in 1955

we have worked on. These include 'White Bear', Knutsford, 'Tollemache Arms' at Taddingley, 'Bowling Green' at Little Leigh, 'Eagle & Child' at Kirkham, 'Legs O Man' at Smallwood, 'White Horse' at Shropham, 'Crown' at Bunwell, 'Queen's Head' at Great Ellingham, 'Chequers' at Bressingham, 'The Bull' at North Lopham, 'King's Head', North Lopham, 'Bleeding Wolf' at Congleton, Cheshire, 'The Smoker' at Plumley, 'The Hob' near Preston.

Stack thatching was gradually decreasing and did not take up much of our time. We reed thatched New Waters Lodge, Wortham, and part of Jacques' Cottage, Garboldisham. These jobs left our reed stock low and we discovered new reed to cut on Hinderclay and Hopton Fens after we had cut our usual crops.

In 1957 we carried out extensive repairs to the reed thatch on Stud Buildings at Exning for Mr B. Van Cutsen, then reed thatched a large boathouse for Lord Fisher of Kilverstone.

At the end of September we were finishing off reed thatching the north side of the Nave end of Old Buckenham church when Father was taken ill. He died on September 26 aged 82.

With the exception of the times when he was thatching away from home, which in his early life was rare, most of those 82 years were spent in Bridgham. I think he not only lived there but was a great part of this small village. I have a draft of the Bridgham, Risley Gawdy Charities dated November 2, 1899, in which he was a trustee, and as previously mentioned, he was almost a permanent member of the Bridgham Parish Council and secretary of many organisations. And what a handy man he had been! I have seen him build up his pony cart wheels, and this included making new 'fellys' and spokes, an expert job for any wheelwright. He was also a very useful cobbler and this was a necessity in our family.

Another part-time activity was the village grave-digging, and he often had a waiting list for his hair-cuts at 1d or 2d for 'outsiders', and in his 'spare time' he cultivated four allotments to provide plenty of vegetables for us and beet for the pony.

Of course he dropped many of these latter activities when our family grew up and left home. The pony and cart were displaced and the extra allotments were not required, but much of the literary work was kept up to his last few days.

One of his transactions in his latter years, which brought full agreement from all the family, was the buying of his house, the old 'White Lion', where we had lived for many years. This assured our sister Enid a home which she richly deserved. She had kept our home together so long after the tragic loss of mother in 1931.

Yes, Tom Reeve, as he was known, was truly missed in Bridgham.

5. B. & J. Reeve, East Harling

John and I went into partnership at once, trading as 'B. & J. Reeve, East Harling', and there could never have been a happier partnership. This lasted until I retired at the end of September 1967.

Leslie carried on alone, his billheads reading 'Thomas Reeve & Sons (L. Reeve), Manchester', and we arranged his supplies of materials from Norfolk as usual.

Before leaving the description of the partnership of John and me too far behind, let me give some of the reasons for the happy combination in our work and play. We were brought up in a home free from family rows and were later dedicated to the craft of our ancestors. We shared the same interests in all kinds of sport, which meant agreement to leave a job if an important match appealed to us. We lived nearly next door, and our families got on well together. At work our employers or customers often marvelled how we worked in unison all the time, but most of this credit should go to John, because it would have been a poor sort of character who could not get along with him.

I always kept the books and sent out the estimates etc. and except for a few casual queries he left everything to me and our accountants. He was a great worker and a first class craftsman, but his easy temperament and his willingness to help others had to be seen or experienced to be believed - the little things like shopping for old people, and where we worked he would clean the old folks' windows, scrape out their chimney pots, get the water from the wells and various odd jobs. But one of the most responsible undertakings was when we were repairing a reed thatched house standing in a lonely part of a village near Thetford. The young lady living there had twin boys about a year old and they were put out in their twins' pram most days near our stack of thatching materials and they (the twins) got used to our company. One day their mother asked John if he would 'keep an eye' on the twins while she went shopping for an hour, and of course John agreed. Things were all right while they had a short 'afternoon nap' but when they woke up and started throwing things out of their pram and insisted on John picking them up, he had to spend the whole afternoon keeping them in order, because it was *three hours* before the mother returned and we were working overtime baby-sitting.

After a cautious year or two we took on bigger and better-priced jobs, but I must mention a small one which was unique in our records. We had a contract job for the Air Ministry in 1958, a small cottage standing on the old airfield (famous for the airships) at Pulham St. Mary. Our estimate for thatching this cottage was £69.16.0. including straw and other materials. This was not accepted and we carried out an alternative repair job for £42.17.0. (for economic reasons).

We had previously thatched churches, lych gates, public houses, pavilions, summer houses, an ice house, aviaries, well tops, garden walls and ornaments, trade signs and bee hives, but in 1960 we reed thatched our first school. It was Les's contract at Penley in Flintshire and was named 'Madras V.P. School', a copy of a missionary school

19. Madras V. P. School, Penley, Flintshire.

56

in Madras founded by the second Lord Kenyon in 1811. This had always been straw-thatched, but the problem of suitable straw decided the owners to accept Les's estimate for reeds. It was quite a job stripping off and carting away the old decayed thatch. John and I loaded the new materials in Norfolk and went for a fortnight to help Les to get most of the roof covered in during the school Easter holiday, and by working long hours we had nearly all the reeds, about 3000 bunches, on the roof before we left for home. Children's playgrounds where we had unloaded the reeds were not suitable places to leave precious materials scattered about during school terms and we were relieved to be able to make such progress before we had to leave.

Later in the year John and I had our first £400 estimate accepted. This was for reed thatching a new bungalow at Barningham, Suffolk. We had previously thatched a cottage for the lady, Mrs Lowe, who had this built to her own specifications, everything built under the cover of the thatch. The roof measured 24 squares, with over 100 feet of ridges, quite a large roof for a bungalow. Unfortunately the old lady died after a fall within nine months of moving into her dream home.

20. Mrs Lowe's dream bungalow, Barningham, Suffolk.

The reeds at Larling were now useless and our local cutting was confined to Hopton and Blo Norton fens. With several big jobs ahead we arranged supplies, with the help of our Association, from Ranworth, Horsey and Freethorpe.

We required 3500 bunches of reeds for another contract with the Thingoe R.D.C. This was four grouped dwellings connected to an existing straw thatched cottage which did not require thatching. The whole group formed a letter H. Here again we had the benefit of the scaffolding by getting on the job early. We fixed all the eaves on the four bungalows before the scaffold was required on another job. Everything turned out satisfactory with the Council this time. Here is the copy of the estimate which we worked to:-

James H. Warren, Architect, 5 Angel Hill, Bury St Edmunds
1961 Thingoe R.D.C. Housing Old Persons' Bungalows, Horringer

42 square reed thatching @ £5	£212. 10. 0.
152 ft ornamental ridge @ 10/-	76. 0. 0.
Norfolk Reeds	330. 0. 0.
Straw for Ridges	18. 0. 0.
Brotches and Rods	16. 10. 0.
Binding Hooks	33. 10. 0.
Binders and Tarred cord	7. 10. 0.
Carting and travelling or lodgings	82. 0. 0.
$\frac{3}{4}$" wire netting and pins	27. 0. 0.
Fixing netting on ridges and ends	10. 10. 0.
Pd	£813. 10. 0.

Thingoe R.D.C. to arrange for ladders.

*****

Flint Cottage, Barningham, was another straw thatched roof we converted to reeds. After the completion of this job we parted with the van father had bought us eight years earlier. We bought another new vehicle and during the remainder of our partnership we changed to a

58

new van every two years, a policy which worked very well.

Banham Fen which we straw-thatched was the scene of my earlier mentioned accident. While I was absent John carried on with the thatching, helped by the owner, Mr Jack Germony, who worked hard at the straw-pulling and serving. I think he was glad when I returned fit and well.

When we thatched with straw, John usually did the 'serving' until we fixed the ridge, when we could both work on the roof. Reed thatching was different, the bundles of reeds were easily prepared by 'bumping' them on a board before we carried and laid them in position on the roof, and we both worked on the sections of roof.

Among the many cottages we thatched in 1962 was Rosemary Cottage, Mundford, in which, it is said, King Charles I slept during 1646. There is also some remarkable carving in the timber over the fire-place in this cottage.

'Rosemary Cottage' reminds me of other delightfully named places we have worked on:-

'This-I-dew' at Rickinghall, 'Hereami' also at Rickinghall, 'Silver Farm House', Besthorpe, 'Frogs Bottom' which I have already mentioned, others like 'Fuchsia Cottage', 'Lilac Cottage', 'Vine Cottage', 'Willow Cottage', 'The Poplars' and 'The Pines' may help someone in selecting a name for their new home.

The winter of 1962-63 was our worst in memory for thatching. We were half way through a job at Coney Weston Hall Farm House (the house mentioned in 1946 records). Extensive improvements and alterations to the roof for a new owner made it necessary to re-thatch in straw. Reed thatching was thought too expensive. Severe frosts started and made the laying of wet straw impossible, except for an occasional hour at mid-day. The job should have taken us about four weeks, but it was eight weeks before we finished, proving how much a part the weather played in our trade.

Then followed the reed-cutting which was completely on ice or in snow. We cut our usual 'beds' then we cut Redgrave 'New Waters', normally too deep to get about on except by boat, and this was the only time we attempted the job. The ice was so thick a tractor and trailer were driven across without any trouble.

During this cold spell Les tried to finish off one of his jobs at Taberley, Cheshire, and had a bad accident. He slipped from the roof and smashed both his ankles, which required several operations during his sixty-two weeks of absence from his work. One foot remains partially disabled but he lost no confidence or skill. However, being self-employed the financial loss must have been felt.

The wintry weather dragged on through March and we started work again on a cottage in North Lopham. According to my diary, there was still very cold easterly winds and on April 5 more heavy snow.

*****

What is it worth to reed thatch a garden bird shelter? John and I were reed-thatching a cottage in Suffolk for a farmer and landowner with sons also in the industry. One of these sons brought a bird shelter from his garden, which he wanted thatched. We brought this home in our van, worked on it during most of that Sunday so that we could return the finished shelter on the Monday morning.

We used ten bunches of reeds, then costing £1, hooks and other materials 10/-. We made no specific charge, but said we would accept a 'good drink' or whatever he thought it was worth.

After a few days consideration we were rewarded with 2/6 each.

*****

When thatching with straw it was our usual practice to leave the cutting of the eaves the last job before fixing the wire netting. When we thatched Silver Farm House, Besthorpe, we decided to cut the overhanging eaves earlier to let more light into the kitchen window which was only a few feet below. This decision probably saved the old house from destruction when an overflowing pan started a fire in the kitchen. The flames which burst through the window would surely have reached the straw if we had not cut off the extra overhanging two feet. The owner, Mr David Thompson, managed to contain the fire in the kitchen, but there was considerable damage. What a shock it would have been for us, after three weeks work on the roof, if we had found the house burned when we arrived for work that morning.

We broke new ground when we reed thatched a cottage at Gislingham, Suffolk. It was rather special because it was next door to a local thatcher, David Fuller, an expert straw thatcher who did not take on any reed work. While we were working there we were often visited by a farmer, Mr A. Smith, who lived nearby, and I suppose he liked the look of our work and our behaviour. Anyway he persuaded us to estimate for straw thatching his group of cottages nearly opposite where we were working. David was already swamped with orders so he had no objections. Mr Smith accepted our estimate, but unfortunately died before we started with the thatching. Mrs Smith carried on the farm business and we completed our contract for which we were promptly paid. Tragedy struck again shortly afterwards when Mrs Smith, a hard working lady who would easily carry a sack of corn, died suddenly and the farm which had been stricken by the earlier death was now left without any family to carry on.

Thatching a house near Attleborough brought us financial anxieties for a few days. Several people in the village said we would be lucky if we got the money for the estimated work. Some thought we were crazy to undertake the job for 'George' who owed some of them money and also others. After four days of uneasiness I decided to ask for 'a little on account'. Imagine my surprise when I got back to the top of the ladder, George was also half way up with £100 in an envelope. There was also a prompt settlement when we finished and we made no secret of this to our earlier informers. However much this information was true we had no complaints and our trust in our customers during the rest of our partnership was never shaken.

At the time of my retirement every work account was settled within two weeks.

Our reed thatching area extended to another village, Walsham-le-Willows, when Mr W. Palfrey, a Suffolk thatcher, partially retired. He was then 77. We converted two straw thatched cottages (Avenue Cottages) to reed thatch. They required some alterations and repairs

21. The author sorting reed

to the wood work, but we were satisfied with the completed job. As usual it 'landed' us on another job or two in the village.

One was 'Four Ashes Cottages' for Mr Martineau. These required extensive work to the timbers, and new windows in the thatch. We had to leave the job at times to allow the carpenter, who was a perfectionist, to get ahead of us. He was still applying his craft to the gable ends, etc., long after we finished.

Bridgham Paddocks barn, often included in our account, was known as Bridgham Field barn in the 1870s, and in the estimates given for thatching the measurements show no alterations to the roof for the last 100 years. The only similarity in the accounts is the time taken for the job. Peter Reeve and 'man' took six weeks in the 1870s for which they were paid £9. We assume the owners supplied the materials, if so it was a reasonable wage compared with the farm workers of those days who were probably working for 10/- per week.

Father's price in 1940 was £49.11.3 including straw etc. but not new wire netting because of the restrictions on this material then being enforced. This time the thatching also took about six weeks.

In 1964 the old roof was in bad condition again when John and I gave it our 'last coat of straw'. Because of the rarity of drum-threshed straw we used rye threshed by a *stationary* combine, and it was quite usable but rather battered. It was supplied by the tenant farmers and the owners supplied the wire netting. We kept a fairly accurate account of the materials we used and the number of brotches was astonishing, nearly 15,000. These were all sharpened at each end, so there was always plenty to do under cover during the worst of the weather. The price, including brotches and other expenses, was £320, but the time, 38 days, compares with previous thatchings.

Copy of an account for September and October 1910:-
    Thomas Reeve
    Straw thatching Bridgham Field barn

43 squares @ 5/6	£11. 19. 3
Ridging 99 ft @ 10d	4. 2. 6
Fixing wire netting over thatch	2. 0. 0
Cost of wire and staples	16. 10. 0.
Pd	34. 11. 9

*****

Thelnetham Lodge Farm House was the largest house we straw thatched, measuring 45 squares with 115 ft ridging, and this cost over £400 excluding straw. The farmer, Dugold (Jock) Ferguson, who lived in the house, supplied the straw and this caused him problems. He carted three loads from several miles away, but when we started thatching we found this unsuitable. We tried other samples but finally used his own straw grown on the field opposite. The house was three storeys high and our own thatching ladders were too short to lay safely on the eaves, so 'Jock' bought an excellent long ladder specially for the job. When we finished we tried to buy the ladder because we had other tall buildings on our waiting list. Jock would not sell, but he offered the ladder on loan whenever we worked on a higher than average roof. We were glad to accept this offer about two years later, and he not only supplied the ladder, he delivered it to the job free. Jock was the most helpful and generous Scot we worked for.

We appreciated the new buildings we thatched because we were spared the stripping off of old thatch which was the worst part of our job. What a problem this caused when we had to pull the rotted thatch off a house standing in a main street or with no back garden in which we could dispose of it by burning. Sometimes there was not even a gate and all the rubbish had to come over the roof. There was the fire risk and the wind could also cause trouble. The old thatch handled cold in the winter, but I think we preferred this to the 'muck and soot' we stirred up during the hot and dry weather. We have gone home from a stripping job looking like sweeps. This was bad enough when we went to our own homes, but more embarrassing when we were in lodgings.

Our method was to take off the old thatch in sections so that any repairs could be done to the rafters. Then we covered the area in again before another stripping. This way we had less roof exposed and the minimum of covering with tarpaulins, but this also caused the stripping to last for more days, and we continued to go home 'filthy' for a longer period.

Straw thatched buildings were the most difficult to strip off. We often found six or seven coats on roofs where the straw thatch had been renewed without thinning the old thatch.

Some of Father's earlier estimates included 'Stripping off old thatch £2' and this often included carting away and burning. Later it was plainly stated, 'Owner to dispose of old thatch.'

Old reed thatch, usually fastened on with tarred rope, was easier to strip. After taking off various thicknesses of ridge we cut through the tarred rope and the reeds would slide down the roof taking the 'muck' with them.

When we later thatched Coney Weston Church we found evidence of four different materials used for binding on the reeds. There were two kinds of blacksmith-made hooks, tarred rope and fen grass rope. The latter was still in good condition after an estimated existence of 200 years.

22. Fen Grass Rope used on Coney Weston Churchin the eighteenth century

6. Last Years of Thatching

We finished with local reed-cutting after 1965 and relied on all our supplies from the Broads. The overall costs were more, but we were able to spend more time on the roofs and we were spared the extra hard work in the cutting. We also knew we were using the best reeds in the country. Les had a book full of orders, so we had no fears of over-buying.

1967, the last year before my retirement, was a hectic year. We arranged our programme to include the largest jobs on the books, because some of these would have been difficult for a lone thatcher. Yet one of the outstanding events in my diary was far away from thatching. It was a football match when Norwich City visited Manchester United in the F.A. Cup.

John and I were supporters of Norwich and our local teams since our playing days. Norwich had a good 'Cup run' in 1959 when we visited Tottenham (twice), Sheffield and Birmingham, but the visit to Manchester which ended in Norwich winning 2-1 seemed the greatest of outings. We met Les, who was naturally a Manchester supporter, and we went to the match together but there was little time to discuss thatching.

It was one of our smallest jobs which probably attracted the most attention to our work. We were reed thatching a porch on a house in Fersfield when we recorded talks on thatching for the B.B.C. in their programme 'The Countryside in January.'

Then we moved to reed thatch 'Fuchsia Cottage', Kenninghall, which had undergone extensive alterations. The old roof had been straw thatched for hundreds of years.

Next we reed thatched sections of the old Blacksmith's Cottage at Gasthorpe for which we cut our own sedge for the ridge, using a borrowed machine; this was the first time we had 'mechanised' this job.

A group of four cottages, Rectory Cottages, Coney Weston, we thatched with straw before our last major job, reed thatching Coney

Weston Church. Perhaps we realised this would be our last major job because we put something special into this work. All the little extras, which our experience found were needed, were put in. The best materials were used. We reinforced many of the 'hazel sways' with thick galvanised wire to ensure the reeds would hold, when in years to come the woodworm attack the sways. We re-battened the roof and we had any suspect rafters replaced. We finished at the end of August and the letters we received showed we had satisfied many people besides ourselves.

23. Coney Weston Church 1967 - the last major thatching job undertaken by B. & J. Reeve

Copy of the estimate for reed thatching Coney Weston Church:-

CONEY WESTON CHURCH

June 28/1967	£ s. d.
18 squares reed thatching @ £10	185. 0. 0
47 feet ridging (ornamental front) @ 16/-	37.12. 0
Reeds and carting	215. 0. 0
Sedge for ridge and carting	12. 0. 0
Hooks and tarred cord	34. 0. 0
Brotches, rods and binders	12. 0. 0
Stripping off old thatch	26. 0. 0
$\frac{3}{4}$" x 48" x 20G wire netting	11. 10. 0
Fixing netting on ridge and ends	10. 0. 0
Travelling expenses	15. 0. 0.
	358. 2. 0.

Church Council to arrange for scaffolding, wood repairs and dispose of old thatch.

*****

We reed thatched an extension to Walnut Tree Farm-House at Tibenham. This adjoined an existing straw thatched roof, which it was hoped would be thatched in reeds by John in the future.

By a strange coincidence the last days of our business partnership were spent ridging Coney Weston Post Office, the same roof on which I started working regular with John in 1946.

*****

On October 1st, 1967, John took over the business as 'J. E. Reeve, East Harling' and I arranged to work two days per week for him, helping him when I was most required and also providing a little petrol money for myself.

He reed thatched the west side roof on Riddlesworth Rectory stables and straw thatched Puddledock Cottage, Old Buckenham. At 'Rose Cottage', North Lopham, he straw thatched the south side and after repairing the north side, he fixed a new ridge and covered the roof with new wire netting. We had two days repairing the straw thatch on the huge Roudham Hall Farm Barn and during the next week we repaired the reed thatch on 'Village Farm House', Market Weston.

After a few other repair jobs he straw thatched the back roof of the 'Butts Cottages', Kenninghall, but his last job was repairing Mrs Gale's house at Kenninghall, February 15, 1968.

John died on May 8 aged 56 and the fact that over 150 people attended his funeral service is proof of the respect held for him. Among those present were representatives of the National Thatchers' Association, the Norfolk Thatchers' Association, the British Legion, all the local sports clubs, and many other organisations to which he had given valuable help. A memorial seat on the Harling Recreation Field given by committee members, and memorial iron gates by the football club are further reminders of his popularity.

Just before my retirement we received one of the most novel requests for our thatching which we just could not refuse to consider in spite of the pile up of orders in the books. This came in the form of a poem, composed and sent by Oriel Sutherland, a famous opera singer, who was very concerned about the state of the thatched roof on 'Hampton House' where her parents, Mr and Mrs Crowe, lived at Blo Norton:-

A Cry from the Heart

The winter is coming,
My parents are old,
They need a stout roofing
To keep out the cold.

The wind and the rain
Beat cruel and fast.
Look at that roof top -
Oh how can it last?

The holes are like craters,
The edges worn thin.
Oh pity the pensioners,
For sure 'tis a sin -

To delay and to tarry
Till Jack Frost descend,
While the old folk have little
Their heads to defend -

Against blast and blizzard,
Against snow and hail.
Hark to my pleading
That now cannot fail.

My thanks to you both
For bending the ear.
Do I see in your eyes
The ghost of a tear?

As you picture that couple
A pale shade of blue
All covered one morning
With wet Norfolk dew.

O.S. '67

In the following April when John was very ill, but we still hoped he would recover, I sent the following estimate on his behalf and it later proved to be the last in the book.

Estimate for straw thatching Hampton House

	£ s. d
20 squares straw thatching @ £7	140. 0. 0
74 ft plain ridging @ 10/-	37. 0. 0
44 ft ornamental front ridge @ 3/- extra	6. 12. 0
Brotches, rods and hooks	24. 5. 0
5 Rolls $\frac{3}{4}$" x 48" 20 G. netting & lacing wire	38. 0. 0
Fixing wire netting	20. 0. 0
Part travelling exs	8. 0. 0
Wheat straw & carting (approx)	45. 0. 0
	318. 17. 0

Owner to dispose of old thatch etc.

After John died a month later this was one of the first jobs I had to cancel. Unfortunately there was some difficulty before another thatcher could be found, but when the work was done with the straw which was acquired for us, the price for the job was about £100 above our estimate.

*****

What happened to the other brothers who had earlier lessons in the thatching trade? Many left, as explained before, to make way for younger brothers or for better financial rewards, but in an emergency any of them would be willing to 'help father out', and all were fully capable.

However, Tom the eldest was not often called upon. He left thatching in 1920 and started driving tractors for an agricultural contractor, W. J. Woods, Thetford, and he drove one of the first Fordson tractors to come into the district. He was later considered an expert at the job and many farmers especially requested his services.

When the Forestry Commissioners took over thousands of acres in the Brecklands, Tom was a specialist at 'drawing' the rows with the double furrows in which they planted the young trees. Thousands of straight lines of large trees are there now to show proof of his skill. Later he became a fitter with other firms at Dereham and Salhouse, and at 70 years old he was still a chargehand in the same trade in Norwich.

Walter left thatching to work on the railways and while a porter at Harling Road Station he enjoyed his job, but he had a different opinion when he was transferred to Manchester. He returned home and started driving road transport and remained in this work, except for the times he was 'borrowed' to help out when thatching jobs piled up. He was on the staff of B.R.S. when he retired with a pension after nearly forty years in transport.

'Peter', who was christened William, inherited this nickname from our thatcher grandfather Peter. He also left thatching for the railways at Harling Road Station, then he was moved to Yarmouth and began to settle down there, but he was later moved to Chingford to become a carriage-cleaner. This was a filthy and unhealthy job in those days. He lodged with a council foreman and eventually married his daughter Hilda. Helped by his father-in-law, Peter soon found employment with the Metropolitan Water Board, starting as a 'navvy' digging trenches etc., and worked his way through various stages until his retirement at 60 with the rank of District Foreman.

John, who is freely mentioned, was the only brother (except me) who did not start in thatching straight from school. He had to do the usual share before leaving school but at 14 he took a shop boy's job at East Harling. John was happy there, especially going the village rounds by horse and cart with Mr Noel Halls, the adult shop assistant, but on reaching the age of 16 his employer would not pay his insurance stamp, so that started his long thatching career.

Leslie had a short time on the farm soon after leaving school when thatching jobs were a little scarce but from 1936, except for his war service in the heavy artillery, he has been a regular thatcher. Strange to say, Les would have preferred a 'flying job' if he had been given the choice. I have heard him talk about his 'unofficial' flights with the Yanks during the Burma Campaign and the Far East. Some of his leaves were spent with them, dropping supplies from the air and flying to India. Since the war he has made many visits to East Anglian Air Displays and Aerodromes. He has also collected some remarkable pieces of history about the Air Forces during the wars, quite a contrast to the old and steady craft which he carried out so well.

It now seems that Leslie, with no successor, will be the last of a long line of thatching Reeves. John's only son showed no interest in the family craft, and my family is one daughter.

Public service appeared to be a part in the life of the three generations I have written about. Peter Reeve was connected with Bridgham Parish Council during the late 19th century. Thomas Reeve held various official posts on the Bridgham Parish Council and many other organisations for fifty years. He was also the founder secretary of the once locally famous Bridgham Show. Walter Reeve followed in Father's footsteps and became a Bridgham Parish Councillor, and sister Enid keeps up the family tradition on committees and helping various causes.

John served on the committees of Harling Branch British Legion, Norfolk Thatchers' Association, Harling Savings Club, Harling Football Club for whom he was competition secretary, and for many years the club linesman.

I served on Harling Parish Council 21 years, and the Harling Recreation Committee, of which I was a founder member, 30 years, and on various local committees.

Looking back over the hard times, the good times, tragedies, comedies and happenings which I have written about, I find I have left many 'date gaps' but I have done my best to put on record how most of our difficulties were overcome without a 'split' in the family, leaving many friends and, we hope, many satisfied owners of thatched roofs.

The only regret is the distant future, when there will be no 'Thatcher' Reeves from Bridgham.

Appendix

Since my retirement I have collected a variety of tools used in bygone days and foremost among them are the thatching tools used by at least three generations of Reeves, spreading over the hundred years. These were shown in an Anglian Television programme 'Bygones' in which I took part on May 1, 1969. A sample of the Fen Grass rope which we found on Coney Weston Church was another exhibit.

Thatchers' tools varied in shape and size, but in principle they were the same, home-made or made by the local blacksmith. The tools used by the Reeve family are illustrated on the early pages of this book and are now in the Gressenhall Museum of Rural Life.